# AUGUSTINE

## THE FARMER'S BOY

## OF TAGASTE

# AUGUSTINE
## THE FARMER'S BOY
## OF TAGASTE

by

### P. DE ZEEUW, J.Gzn

**INHERITANCE PUBLICATIONS**
**NEERLANDIA, ALBERTA, CANADA**
**PELLA, IOWA, U.S.A.**

**Canadian Cataloguing in Publication Data**
Zeeuw, P. de
 Augustine, the farmer's boy of Tagaste
   Translation of: De Boerenjongen van Thagaste

  ISBN 0-921100-05-1

  1. Augustinus, Saint, Bishop of Hippo—Juvenile literature. 2. Christian
saints—Algeria—Hippo—Biography—Juvenile literature. I. Title.
BR1720.A9Z43 1988     j270.2'092'4     C88-091442-4

**Library of Congress Cataloging-in-Publication Data**
Zeeuw, P. de
   [Boerenjongen van Thagaste. English]
  Augustine, the farmer's boy of Tagaste / P. de Zeeuw.
     p.    cm.

  Summary: Presents a biography of Augustine of Hippo, who grew up during
the decay and fall of the Roman Empire and whose writings had particular
significance to Christians and their church at this time.
  1. Augustinus, Saint, Bishop of Hippo—Juvenile literature. 2. Christian
saints—Algeria—Hippo (Extinct city)—Biography. I. Title.
BR1720.A9Z4413 1998
270.2'092—dc21
[B]

                                                      98-37869
                                                          CIP
                                                           AC


5th Printing 2018

ISBN 978-0-921100-05-8

Translated from the Dutch by M.F. Woonings
Cover design by Bart Oost
Illustrations by Hein Kray

3317 Township Rd 624 (4.5 miles north of Neerlandia, .5 mile west)
County of Barrhead, AB T0G 1R1 Canada
Tel. 780-674-3949
Web site: inhpubl.net
E-Mail: orders@inhpubl.net

Published simultaneously in U.S.A. by Inheritance Publications
Box 366, Pella, Iowa  50219

Available in Australia from Inheritance Publications
Box 1122, Kelmscott, W.A. 6111  Tel. (089) 390 4940

Printed in Canada

# TABLE OF CONTENTS

# INTRODUCTION

You must never think of Augustine as Roman Catholic. He belonged to the one, at that time undivided, universal Christian Church and indeed fought against Roman Catholic deviations. Many unscriptural ideas had as early as the fourth century crept into the Christian Church. Yet many of her members continued in the desire to serve the Lord faithfully, according to His Word. They warned against heresies and ungodly practices.

One of the men who stood for the scriptural truth and defended it against many heretics was Augustine. Therefore it is right that you should know him as one of the great teachers of the Christian Church, next to Martin Luther and John Calvin.

Augustine was born on November 13, A.D. 354.

P. de Zeeuw, J.Gzn.,
*Nijkerk (the Netherlands)*

# CHAPTER ONE

## "WHERE HAVE THE PEARS GONE?"

The whip in the teacher's hand swept through the air and came to a sudden stop on the back of Augustine, who was yet again pulling one of his stunts. The boy cried out in pain. It was not the first lashing of the morning either. He had received several already.

Augustine was at a complete loss.

Last night he had prayed! His mother, the pious Monica, had told him that prayer always helped. Augustine did not really believe it for one minute. He preferred to agree with his father Patricius, who found it much easier to remain a heathen. But after he had been hit by the teacher every single day, he thought it wise to try his mother's suggestion about praying. What if he asked the Lord to stop him from being hit so often? It might just mean the end of all his troubles! He had stuck to his plan, and last night in bed he had told the Lord all about his problem.

This morning he had gone to school in good spirits. Now it would all be different! "Prayer works!" That was what his mother told him, and she should know. Did she not always attend the church in Tagaste? She even prayed at home. She was a God-fearing woman. His father Patricius laughed about her faith, but he never stopped her.

As it turned out, his mother had not known at all!

As the whip landed on his back a few more times, the boy decided never to pray again. After all, it had done him no good whatsoever. In fact, this morning he had been given even more lashes than usual! No, prayer was not for him. He was convinced of that.

When Augustine looked around he saw only grinning faces. Apparently the other students were of the opinion that he deserved all he had been given. Well, they would find out. As soon as he could, Augustine would get even with them!

His mother asked him, "How is it Augustine, that you are always getting punished at school, while your elder brother Navigius is hardly ever in trouble?"

"Navigius is a goody-goody. He always does exactly what the teacher says," the boy had answered.

"That is what you should do too."

"I can't. I hate school. I would much rather be outside in the fields."

"But my dear, that won't work. You need your education. You have to learn something."

"I know, but it takes much too long. It is always the same, again and again. And I already know it all."

Mother Monica sighed deeply.

It was all true. If Augustine read a psalm just once, he was able to repeat it by heart. He was a very fast learner. That was why he disliked school so much.

When the boy came home that evening, he screamed: "I never want to go back to school! I think it is a prison for slaves—a hole!"

Up to a point the boy was right. What was called a school was in fact no more than a rough shelter. Old tarpaulins protected the children from sun or rain while they sat on rickety stools or discarded, worn-out mats. The place really was boring, and if on top of that you were lashed every day, you would soon be fed up.

That night Augustine lay awake for a long time. He just had to do something, but what? Prayer was out! He knew all about that! Staying away from school seemed the best thing to do, but would it be possible? Certainly not if father Patricius was home. His father was a kind of gentleman-farmer who did very little more than watch his slaves, hunt, ride his horse, and generally make sure that he was indeed a gentleman. He was also one of Tagaste's city councillors.

When Augustine finally fell asleep, it was with a vague plan to stay away from school if the opportunity presented itself.

That is exactly what happened.

When he arose the next morning, he heard from the house-slaves that his father had left earlier and would be away hunting all that day. Certainly a step in the right direction. Then his sister told him that Mother had gone into the city to visit the poor. She often did that. Although Patricius was not really wealthy, his wife always managed to save something in order to help the poor. When she did that, she walked through the entire city. So now the coast was clear!

No school. No lashes!

His day was suddenly a lot brighter.

The only question was, what would he do all day? He liked playing in the street, but that was a bit dangerous right now. Just imagine what would happen if Mother Monica saw him? No, better go into the fields. The house was surrounded by orchards, and with a few of his friends, he set out on his adventure.

They had lots of fun, but their boisterous activities made them hungry, and they wanted something to eat badly. That something was not hard to find, because the trees were laden with fruit. Suddenly the truants discovered a tree full of the most delicious looking pears, the kind you never saw in Tagaste. That was not strange, because father Patricius had cultivated them himself. He had already calculated that they would bring a pretty penny, because they were indeed beautiful, juicy pears. But now the boys had discovered them.

Before long, two or three of them had reached the top of the tree. Augustine knew that it was his father's favourite tree, but he said nothing. In fact, he joined in. They picked pears until the tree was empty. Than they began to eat them, continuing until they could not look at another pear. Afterwards they fed the leftovers to the pigs.

That was it. They'd had a wonderful day: plenty of pears, no lashes, it couldn't have been better!

In the evening when Patricius had come home from his hunting trip, he went for a walk in the orchard. The weather had been warm, but under the trees it was now lovely and cool. He decided to have another look at his pear tree. He would have the pears picked tomorrow. They should be ready now and must not become overripe.

He looked up into the tree.

What was that?

Not a single pear left in the whole tree!

"Where have the pears gone?" he murmured. Had one of the slaves picked them already? it was quite possible that Monica had ordered them to be picked. Walking slowly, he left the orchard. He passed the shed and decided to look in on the pigs. He went toward the cages and slipped on a chewed pear. Then he saw more pears in the feeding troughs. Evidently the pigs had not been able to eat all of them. He took one of them in his hand–but this was a pear of his special tree! Patricius felt his anger rising and became suspicious. What if Augustine played that trick on him? He could hardly believe it, but if he had, the boy would certainly know about it!

As soon as he came inside, he asked Monica where Augustine was.

"He has just gone to bed. But Patricius, what is wrong?" She could see that he was terribly angry, and she feared that once again Augustine had been up to no good.

"Nothing! I only want to ask him what has happened to the pears!"

"The pears? Which pears do you mean?"

"They are gone! The whole tree, empty. And the pears are in the pig troughs."

"Oh, but that is terrible!"

Patricius heard no more. He had grabbed a stick and was storming upstairs.

Augustine heard him coming and pretended to be asleep, but it was no use!

"Wake up, you!" yelled his father, while at the same time painfully introducing him to the stick. "What have you done with my beautiful pears?"

"Ouch!" Augustine cried, "I have eaten them, Father."

"Oh yes, eaten them and given them to the pigs! Out of bed with you!"

His father continued to wield the stick, and in no time at all, Augustine was standing next to his bed looking at his father. Mother was standing behind him.

"Patricius," she cried, "no more hitting, please! You could really hurt him!"

Patricius took no notice. He was far too angry to pay any attention to his wife's pleadings.

"Tonight you will not sleep in a bed, understand?"

"Yes Father."

"But what is the boy going to do?" asked Mother Monica in a fearful voice.

"He can sleep with his friends. He and the pigs have eaten my pears! Come on! Off to the shed with you!"

As soon as he knew what his father wanted, he was off! He raced down the stairs, out of the house, and into the shed. There he spent the night huddled under some straw in the farthest corner of the cages.

His mother tried to have the punishment changed, but nothing worked. Patricius was determined to cure his son once and for all of eating his prize pears!

CHAPTER TWO

# SCHOOL BOY IN MADAURA

"You're cheating, Augustine!"

"That's a lie, Levinus!"

"Well, I never! I saw with my own eyes that you hid the nut in your hand! Let me see!"

Augustine opened his hand, but no nut—only a small black mark.

"See!" insisted Levinus, "that is where you held the pitch ball. It has left a dirty mark on your hand!"

The boys were sitting on the stairs built along the outside of a house. They were playing a game called "Find the Nut". On one of the steps were three nutshells with a small lump of pitch, taking the place of a nut, in the middle.

They hunched around the shells and watched eagerly as agile hands quickly took the pitch and hid it under one of the shells. The others had to guess under which shell it had been hidden, but if the player hid the pitch in his hand, they would of course always guess wrong. That is what Augustine had done. Levinus was the first one to notice and yelled out: "You're cheating, Augustine!"

Augustine had won many games by cheating, but now that he had been exposed he was furious! Quick as a flash he hit Levinus in the face and Levinus promptly hit him back. The boys quickly took sides, but most of them were against Augustine because he had cheated. That is why he went home with a bloody nose and other painful reminders of the fight.

Go home—but not to mother Monica. He now lived

14

in Madaura, an ancient Numidic city, where Maximus, an old friend of his father had taken him in.

After the episode with the pears, both Augustine's father and mother had realized that things could not continue the way they were. Augustine could not remain in Tagaste. He would have to go somewhere else. They decided to sent him to Madaura, only a few miles from Tagaste. That was not too far, and when Maximus had promised to give him a home, things had been quickly organized. He would attend the Latin school in Madaura. On a beautiful autumn morning, Augustine, mounted on his horse, had ridden to his new home town.

Monica had been loath to see the twelve-year-old boy go. What would become of him? Oh, if only she could go with him, but that was impossible. Her duties were to her husband and the rest of the family here in Tagaste. Prayer was the only thing left to her now, and pray for Augustine she did! Every day! She knew Madaura. It was a place of sinful heathen people. There were also heathen temples in Madaura. Certainly Maximus would keep an eye on him, but would that be enough?

Studying posed no problem for Augustine. He thoroughly enjoyed it. Here he could really show his teachers what he could do, but studying did not take up all of his time. He spent much of it playing games, particularly "Find the Nut". You could win quite a bit with that, especially if you cheated. All he had won today however was a thrashing and a bloody nose. If he ever got hold of that Levinus!

When the boy arrived home, Maximus asked him what had happened.

"Fought with Levinus. That rat!"

"Ah, Levinus! Yes, he has a strong pair of hands!

Who started, August? Naturally not you!"

"Of course not!"

"But why would he beat you like this? Wait a minute. I'll go see him and give him a piece of my mind. We cannot have him going around giving innocent boys bloody noses; what does he think he's doing?"

Maximus began to walk to the door, but that was exactly what Augustine did not want. He was sure that Levinus would expose him, so he said, "Never mind, he became upset over the game."

"Which game?"

"Find the Nut."

"Ah, now I see! You cheated did you? Yes, yes, I thought so! Levinus may be rough, he is not a cheat! That is what you are, Augustine! Of course he became angry, and I suppose this fight was the result?"

"Yes, that's about it!"

"Well, I shall personally go and thank Levinus. He has done you a favour, boy! Cheating is low, and the sooner you stop it, the better it will be for everyone, including yourself! Now go to bed before I give you a taste of my hands also!"

Augustine looked at his landlord. Was he serious? Yes, he could see in his eyes that he was, and before Maximus could put his threat into action, Augustine had fled to his room! Once there he was so preoccupied with the thought of taking revenge on Levinus that he forgot to pray.

That was not the first time either! He had made a solemn promise to Mother Monica that he would pray each evening before going to bed, but often his mind was so busy with Latin essays, games, or like right now, plans of vengeance, that he completely forgot about prayer. That night he thought for a long time about how he would get even with Levinus, and when he finally did fall asleep, he had it all worked out!

It was a few days later.

On a large block of granite, in a field outside Madaura, stood Augustine. Several schoolchildren were grouped around him, listening attentively to what he had to say.

"Men of Carthage," he began, "Listen to your leader Hannibal, who has always led you to victory! Over there you can see the armies of your archenemies, the Romans. Their leader is the treacherous Scipio. We fear him not! Are we not Carthaginians? We shall totally destroy the Romans, and Scipio will hang from the highest tree!"

The boys smiled. Most of them knew only too well why their leader was so violently opposed to Scipio. The boy playing the role of Scipio was none other than Levinus, who, only a few days before had given Augustine such an unmerciful beating.

Augustine concluded his speech with "Long live Carthage! Let all join in the battle and destroy Scipio and the Romans!"

The armies advanced, and soon the boys were engaged in a very real battle.

Augustine, however, took little notice of that. He and a few friends had arranged to capture Levinus and give him the beating of a lifetime, and so it happened.

Augustine and his friends forced their way through the fighting hordes, and before Levinus realized it, he was surrounded by enemies. Ten against one! A cowardly trick, but Augustine hardly could care less. He was going to get even with Levinus for his bloody nose. He was out for revenge, and he would stoop to anything to get it. In a wink, Levinus was on the ground, with fists raining down on his body, face, and legs from all directions. This cowardly attack made the boy furious, but he was in no position to do anything about it; he was completely overpowered. Augustine's fist landed in the middle of his face; blood gushed from his nose.

"That's for you," he sneered, "and remember, one thing is forever true: You hit me and I'll hit you!"

Levinus screamed, more in frustration than in pain, but in the ruckus, none of his friends noticed that he was in trouble.

Suddenly things changed. The "Romans" looked for "Hannibal" and immediately saw the group of boys attacking Levinus. They all rushed to his aid, and when they saw how he had been manhandled, their fury knew no bounds. They tore the clump of boys apart and grabbed Augustine by his hair. They had suddenly realized the real purpose of this battle, and now the great "Hannibal" was really in for a thrashing. They did not stop until his nose was bleeding as well. Then they topped it off with a black eye!

Beaten, bleeding, and with his clothes in tatters, Augustine arrived back at Maximus' house and there received a second punishment! He was sent to bed without a meal and barred from playing outside for a whole week.

However, that was not all. Augustine's teacher became involved too, because Levinus complained of his cheating and about his unfair attack during their war game. Augustine was severely punished, and only diligence, displayed in his schoolwork, prevented him from being permanently expelled from school.

School was the only thing he enjoyed, and he studied very hard. Especially in Virgil (a Latin poet) he was well versed. He knew many of his works by heart. He even read in bed and many times Maximus had to pull the books from his hand, as he had also done at meal times.

So it went on for a good three years. Diligent study, playing, fighting, and then it was all over! Augustine was honoured as top student, and his teachers had nothing but praise for his work.

He then returned to Tagaste, nearly sixteen years old.

# CHAPTER THREE

## URCHIN IN TAGASTE

"Are you crying, Monica?"

It was after midnight, and Patricius suddenly woke up from a peaceful sleep.

"But why? Why? I would have expected you to be happy now that your beloved son has come home to stay! What else do you want?"

"That is just it. The boy has come home, but how? As a complete pagan. He appears to remember nothing at all of what I have told him about the Saviour. If he continues in that way, he will be lost forever." And again she began to cry.

"Come, come Monica. You don't have to cry. The boy finished his studies as the top student, and he is not yet sixteen. Who knows where his great intelligence will lead him?"

"That is all very well, Patricius," lamented Monica, "but Scripture says, 'What does it profit a man if he wins the whole world but loses his own soul?'"

Patricius sighed heavily. He was no longer so sure about his own gods. He had begun to realize that serving them was a rather empty practice. He tried to comfort his wife: "Maybe things are not as bad as they seem. Let us go to sleep now, and it will all look different in the morning. It was his first day home, and naturally he was excited, but that will change."

Soon after Patricius was asleep. Even Monica, in spite of her fears, managed to doze off.

It was during the following days that she was proven right. Augustine had nothing to do. He knew nothing about working on the farm. He no longer needed to study, so all that was left to do was loaf around. Oh, if only there were enough money!

Patricius refused to listen to Monica's laments about Augustine's pagan ways. He had enough troubles of his own! As well as being a gentleman-farmer, he was a member of the Tagaste city council. The position did not bring in any money, and his farm was becoming more and more disorganized. Yet he dearly wanted to let his son study at the College in Carthage, the capital city. He was certain that if that could be achieved, a glorious future would await Augustine. All the upper-class families in Numidia sent their sons there, and Patricius did not want to appear less than they. But oh, the money! Studying in Carthage was very expensive, and Patricius could not afford it. He wanted to try borrow the money, then Augustine could pay it back himself when he had completed his studies. But who would lend it to him?

While father Patricius was wracking his brains to find the money and mother Monica continually prayed for him, the son went on his own merry way. He befriended the wrong kind of boys and wandered around the city with them, constantly up to no good! Sometimes he did not even bother to come home at night. His favourite pastimes were hunting, horses and gambling. The rest of the time he spent eating and sleeping.

He had also started to date girls and then deceive them. His whole life had become a series of idle days.

Monica admonished him every day with tears in her eyes. She spent half her nights praying for the salvation of her child, but it looked as if the Lord did not hear her.

"You should go and pay Alypius a visit, August," she said one day. "You used to be inseparable when you were younger. He has become a very nice young man. Really, you should go and see him!"

Augustine laughed at the idea. I want nothing to do with that goody-goody," he said. "He is a perfect mother's boy. Too scared to do anything exciting. He doesn't gamble, he doesn't drink, he wants nothing to do with girls! No Mother, you can have him!"

Monica shook her head.

"You need a friend like Alypius," she said. "He would keep you from many a foolish act."

Augustine hugged his mother and gave her a resounding kiss.

"You are the best mother in the world," he said, "and I love you a lot, but you have no idea what a boy like me needs." And that was it! Augustine let his father worry about how to get enough money to pay for his studies, and he let his mother pray for him and cry over him while he continued on living for fun and pleasure.

The people of Tagaste often discussed Augustine's way of life and sometimes judged him rather harshly.

"Monica really had no business marrying a heathen," they said. "It just goes to show you. Look how the boy takes after his father. He is a complete heathen, and Monica with all her piety cannot do a thing about it."

Monica herself did not agree with these people, because she knew that the prayers of the righteous can work much, and she steadfastly continued to pray for her son. Everyday she brought her sorrows to the Lord and asked Him to bring her son to repentance. Oh, if only he would confess his faith in the Lord. Then he could be baptized.

In those days, newborn children were not baptized. It was done at the time of their profession of faith; that is why Augustine, even at his age, had not yet been baptized.

In the meantime, Patricius asked all his friends and acquaintances to lend him money for Augustine's education, but every time it came to nothing; all his efforts had been in vain. One day he said to his wife, "Mother, what would you think if I approached the mayor?"

"Would Romanianus lend you the money?" asked Monica.

"I really don't know, but I can at least try. He is my last hope. If he cannot help me, then I am afraid we shall have to forget about Augustine's further education."

"Well, the mayor is rich enough," answered Monica. "He could certainly help us if he wanted to. Oh, Patricius, I do hope he will! Our son would again have a goal, something to live for. For one whole year he has done nothing but please himself and has spent his days in idleness and indulgence. That will have to stop as soon as possible!"

Patricius wholeheartedly agreed and left to pay Mayor Romanianus a visit. The mayor was extremely wealthy and very generous. He loved to help people, not primarily because of their need, but because he liked being seen as a caring man. People then talked about him and praised him for his generosity. So actually all his generosity was, was self-indulgence. Of course that was not a good reason, but at least people were helped out of trouble. That was also what Patricius thought. He told the mayor that his boy was such a bright student and that he had graduated from the Latin school in Madaura before he had even been sixteen years old as the best student in the school. If the mayor would be willing to lend Patricius the money for his son's education, then almost certainly Augustine would one day be a great man, thanks to Mayor Romanianus.

The idea appealed to the mayor. If in a few years time there were a great man in Numidia telling everyone, "I owe it to Mayor Romanianus that I am where I am today," the people would surely praise him even more! It was praise of the people that the mayor craved, even though it meant very little.

"How much money would you need Patricius?"

"Oh, then you will lend it to me, sir?"

"Certainly I will lend it to you! It would be such a waste if a boy like your son could not finish his education because he lacked money. Just tell me how much you need."

Poor Patricius had become so used to being refused that he had not even thought of an exact amount, and now the mayor suddenly allowed him to name his price.

"Well," he stammered, "the study in Carthage will cost a lot of money."

"Well, certainly it does, and the boy should not

have to scrimp and scratch either. You name the amount."

Just in time, Patricius realized that he would only be borrowing the money and that borrowed money must always be paid back. So he named a very modest sum.

But Romanianus would not hear of it and offered to pay for everything and never mentioned repayment.

.

CHAPTER FOUR

## STUDENT AT CARTHAGE

Patricius was elated when he returned home. He called out to his wife, "It worked, Monica, it worked! The mayor has offered to pay for everything. How about that?"

"Patricius! Will he really do that? It is almost too good to be true!"

"Yes, I felt exactly the same way. Nevertheless, it is true!"

"Oh, I am so happy! How can we possibly thank the Lord for this great blessing?"

"We had better first thank our benevolent Romanianus," suggested Patricius.

Monica realized that her husband did not understand her in these matters, so she ignored his remark.

At seventeen years of age, Augustine set out for Carthage to complete his education. The old Carthage had been destroyed by Scipio, but from its ruins a grand and splendid city had risen.

This city offered a variety of many amusements

that the people in Tagaste had never even imagined. As soon as Monica's joy over the mayor's generosity had subsided, she began to feel great concern for her boy. She knew that the temptations in Carthage would be even greater than in Madaura. Carthage had many heathen temples including one for the great Saturn. This was just the Roman name for the terrible old Phoenician god Moloch, to whom living children were offered up as a sacrifice. There was also a temple for the mysterious Egyptian god Scarpis.

Once Monica realized all this, she almost wished that her son would remain in Tagaste, but of course that was impossible. Romanianus had offered to pay for his studies, and now he simply had to go to Carthage.

Augustine himself was very excited about going. Although he loved his mother a great deal, the idea of living far away from her appealed to him very much.

Once in Carthage, he was awestruck by the city. He had never seen anything like it. Besides a theatre, there was also an odeum[1], a circus, a stadium, and an amphitheater.

A wide scope of entertainment. Everyday a new possibility. Carthage also had its Roman thermal baths, which Augustine and his friends often visited. In no time at all he had made many friends, but they were not the kind mother Monica would have approved of. They lived only for pleasure. However, there were also several Christian churches in Carthage, and it is certain that Augustine visited some of them, but definitely not often. He often came in contact with different heretics. It appeared

---

[1] A kind of opera house, or play-house, where musicians and poets performed.

that Monica's worries were not unfounded, and she faithfully continued to pray for her son every day.

There was Augustine, on his own in this woefully corrupt city of Carthage. Apart from seeking amusement, however, he did study; indeed he studied very hard. He had to–the mayor had not paid for him just to enjoy himself. He took his studies very seriously indeed. He had a goal. He wanted to become just as wealthy as Mayor Romanianus.

He was very good at his studies, and before long he had, as student of the rector whose lectures he attended, attained the position of "major", which not only meant he was top of the class but also leader and prefect over all his friends.

The art of oratory was his greatest love, but he studied music and various forms of mathematics with equal ease. Once his studies were completed, he hoped to become one of Africa's most famous lawyers. To him that seemed the surest and shortest way to fame and fortune.

Then one day he received a letter from his mother saying that his father had suddenly died. She mourned and missed him terribly, but she was very happy to be able to tell Augustine that he had died as a Christian. Shortly before his death, he had confessed his faith in the Saviour and had been baptized.

None of that interested Augustine very much. All he wanted to know was if his father's sudden death would put a stop to his studies. That was very well possible, as Patricius' estate was in rather a mess. Mother Monica, however, put her foot down about that! Come what may, she insisted that her son complete his studies. Even if it meant existing on a crust of bread, she would pay Augustine's board and lodgings. Maybe the mayor would assist her in this, but in any case, Augustine was to remain a student in Carthage.

Augustine would have regretted it very much if his father's death had forced him to leave Carthage. He had just begun to feel at home and enjoy himself. And what would he do about Lepida, the

friendly girl he saw frequently who always answered his courteous greeting with a lovely smile? Very discreetly he had tried to find out more about her, and he had learned that she regularly attended the Christian church services. When he heard that, he also went to church. Not to hear the sermon, oh no! He went to see more of the lovely Lepida. Sometimes he even succeeded in finding a place near her. He would then put little notes in her hand, and they would arrange to meet somewhere. This was very wrong of Augustine, as that is certainly not the purpose of the church services, but he could hardly have cared less. It would be years before he was to realize his wrongdoing and heartily regret it, but right then Augustine was unrepentant. After all, he studied very hard. Surely that entitled him to some fun; he would only be young once!

It was a pity that his friendship with Lepida was far from being enough for Augustine. He wanted rather more than friendship, and he got it! One day he met a student who asked him to become a member of his club.

"What kind of club do you mean?" asked Augustine. "I don't know of any club."

"You do not know about the club of the immoralists?" asked the student. "Man, don't you like having fun?"

"I certainly do!"

"Well, then, you should join our club. We are called the 'Turn-Abouts.' Come on, I'll introduce you!"

Eagerly Augustine went with his newfound friend, who took him to what was called a winehouse where the club had a private room. When the other members heard that Augustine wanted to join the club, he was welcomed with enthusiastic cheers. They had all heard enough about him to understand that he would be just right for their club. They certainly had use for someone who was prepared to fool around and play tricks on people.

They asked him if he went to church. No, he did not believe in that kind of life. He went there only to see a pretty girl he knew.

That remark was greeted with shouts of laughter. He was exactly the man they wanted. They could be assured of having fun with him around, but Augustine realized that the Turn-Abouts were among a group of clubs specifically forbidden for students.

Should the prefect of police hear about it they could be in considerable trouble, so he was to tell no one about it, not even Lepida.

Augustine promised readily. He was quite prepared to promise a whole lot more if it meant that he could join this fun-loving club! It turned out that he had joined the club just in time. Tomorrow they would have a dinner party here in the room and plan a new adventure. How and what, they did not know yet, but Augustine would hear about it tomorrow.

He was so excited about his club membership that he completely forgot the date he had arranged with Lepida for that night.

## CHAPTER FIVE

## "AUGUSTINE, YOU OUGHT TO BE ASHAMED"

It was still early in the afternoon when Augustine arrived at the club room. A few other members had come in ahead of him, and they made him feel very welcome indeed.

When all the others had arrived, the meal was served and a great deal of wine was consumed with it!

Augustine felt very much at ease in this happy

group. They told jokes one after the other, and when they had eaten and drunk their fill, they began to make plans for their next adventure. In the city lived an old professor who was no longer able to see or hear properly, and they decided to play a trick on him. He was the perfect target, because his lectures always went on into the late afternoon. The plan was carefully worked out. Some of the club members even planned to wear disguises. They found things that would create plenty of noise, and armed with these things they went to the old professor's lecture room.

They banged on the door to announce their arrival.

The old professor could barely hear, but that kind of noise startled him.

Alarmed, he turned toward the door, which at that very moment was flung open and the entire horde of singing, screaming troublemakers came in, making the poor man believe that they were after his life. Paralyzed with fear, he fell, chair and all, to the floor.

The Turn-Abouts roared with laughter and began ransacking everything in sight, Augustine willingly assisting them in their destruction. Just look at the students! Most of them fled at the first opportunity, but some brave ones had enough courage to defend themselves against the scoundrels.

A fierce fight began in which the professor took many blows while he tried to get to his feet.

Suddenly Augustine felt himself being firmly gripped by the shoulder and shaken violently.

"Augustine, you ought to be ashamed!" he was told.

He looked rather surprised at the young man

who had attacked him, and just as he got ready to punch him very hard, he recognized Alypius, his former friend from Tagaste.

"You are here, Alypius," he stammered.

"As you see," was the curt reply. "And I am wondering what Mayor Romanianus would say if he could see you right now! The poor man would be better served by throwing his money in the ocean! Come with me immediately! I have brought a letter from your mother."

Augustine had suddenly been brought back to reality. The prank no longer seemed funny to him, and meekly he followed Alypius to his lodgings.

"I had no idea you were here, Alypius," he said.

"I have only just arrived. Father has finally been able to scrape the money together, and now I can study here. I had hoped to be guided by you, but now I see that all you can teach me is how to be a scoundrel."

"Come on Alypius, don't be a spoil sport." Augustine tried to defend his actions. "Surely students are allowed some fun?"

"Oh, I agree. But if you call scaring an old man half to death, fun, then I am afraid your idea of fun is quite different from mine. Again Augustine, you ought to be ashamed of yourself! Oh, and here is your mother's letter."

While reading the letter, Augustine's face fell. This was not a cheerful letter. Naturally, mother began by writing about the temptations of the big city. Although he lived far away from Tagaste, Monica occasionally heard things about her son that caused her grave concern.

"I pray every day that the Lord might turn you from your sinful ways," she wrote, "and I cry myself to sleep over you every single night."

Augustine knew all about that. Mother had never done anything other than pray and cry on his account, but it never changed anything. Here in Carthage he had learned about the teachings of Mani[2], and these teachings suited him just fine. He had now become, and wanted to remain, a Manichaean.

A little further in the letter he found something really disturbing. Mother's finances were rather low, and Mayor Romanianus no longer seemed so eager to help.

If somehow or other the money could not be found, Augustine would have to return to Tagaste.

---

[2] Mani was a Persian philosopher who had started a religion of Persian paganism mixed with a few ideas from Christianity. He wanted to prove that man's reason is superior to God's revealed truth.

"Can you tell me what your mother has written?" asked Alypius. Augustine told him everything.

"But Augustine, that can't be true!"

"O yes it is! Mother says that there is no more money."

"What a terrible shame. I was so hoping to come here and learn from you, but after what I saw tonight, I am not so sure. Really Augustine, you ought to be ashamed. In Tagaste your mother is scrimping and saving for your education, and all you do is befriend louts who waste their time and money. Does it have to be like that?"

"What else can I do?"

"Come now Augustine, you are clever enough to earn some extra money. There are always students who find the work difficult. You could coach them, and if there is a poetry competition, you could send in your work. You could easily win, and it would give you enough money to remain here!"

Augustine became excited. He had never thought of such a solution.

The first thing he did was to resign from the Turn-Abouts. Alypius had been right. He felt ashamed at having been a member of such a club.

He began to write poetry, which sold well, and when there was a poetry competition, he sent in his work and won the prize.

In the meantime, Alypius had found some students who wanted Augustine to coach them. He himself enrolled first and was followed by Hebridus, Horatius, and others.

Augustine wrote his mother a cheerful letter to tell her that he had been able to find work and was now earning enough money so that she no longer had to sent him so much. However, he did not answer his mother's fearful questions. He had no intention of becoming a Christian. He wanted to remain faithful to the teachings of Manichaeus.

The time when Monica no longer needed to pray for her son or shed tears on his behalf was still a long way off.

## CHAPTER SIX

## MONICA EXPELS HER SON FROM HER HOUSE

Mayor Romanianus' son was giving his father a great deal of trouble. No matter what his father did or said, Licentius absolutely refused to study. Something just had to be done. The boy needed a firm hand. Licentius had attended every school in the entire region of Tagaste, and he had been expelled from each of them. The poor mayor was at his wit's end.

Then, suddenly, he had an idea. He remembered the clever Augustine in Carthage.

The mayor had heard that the young man had finished his studies and was now a professor. He was convinced that the farmer's son would still be short of money, because the competition in Carthage was much too great. Here in Tagaste it would be much easier. What if Augustine opened a Latin school here? He could then take on Licentius and keep an eye on him. When the mayor asked Monica about his plan, she wholeheartedly approved. Her boy would once again live under her roof. She could again watch over him, and maybe now he would listen to her. Oh God was good to make this possible! She thanked the Lord for causing Romanius to think of this plan.

Augustine did come to Tagaste. He could hardly do anything else. He would have starved in Carthage, but Tagaste meant a decent living.

There had been things that kept him from wanting to go. He would have to say goodbye to Lepida. He promised the girl that he would return soon, but he knew in his heart that it would actually be a long time before he could come back. Then there was his mother. He loved her very much, but he had absolutely no time for her piety. He was now a Manichaean, and that religion suited him well.

Manichaeus taught that both good and evil have an equal right to existence, and that idea greatly appealed to Augustine.

So the clever son returned to his mother's house. He was made very welcome. Monica embraced and kissed him with tears in her eyes, but before long Augustine realized that his mother had become even more pious than before. She attended church every day, and life at home was governed by strict Christian principles. Now, however, her wayward son had come to upset this peaceful life. Monica could not approve of the friends he constantly brought home, and he generally lived like a heathen. He never prayed, and the idea of going to church never entered his mind. This caused Monica much sorrow.

The school ran perfectly, and Licentius had never learned as much as he did now with Augustine. Romanianus was delighted and paid Augustine a handsome salary.

Monica appreciated the fact that she no longer had to send money to Carthage, but she still had to pray for her son. If only he would fear the Lord, then her happiness would know no bounds. But that was not the case.

Monica decided to tackle her son about it, and one evening, when both were sitting under the lemon tree in the courtyard she said, "Why don't you come to church with me tomorrow, Augustine? Our bishop can explain the Scriptures beautifully."

"No time and, well, no inclination either!"

"But son, that can't go on forever! You are old enough to realize that man cannot live without the Lord. The Saviour has paid for all our sins and reopened the way to the Father."

"You sound like the bishop himself, Mother," laughed Augustine.

"Please Augustine, don't mock. I am indeed serious; every day I pray for your salvation."

"Not necessary Mother! I'll tell you something. In Carthage I became a Manichaean."

This terrible news caused his mother to cry out, "Augustine, no! It can't be true. Please tell me it isn't true—that you want nothing to do with these pagan ideas!"

"If I did that I would be lying, and you always taught me that that is wrong!"

Monica realized that she could not convince her son and decided not to mention it again. Maybe he was pretending to be a Manichaean just to tease her.

That night she did not sleep.

Augustine had not pretended!

That became quite evident when he began to invite other Manichaeans to his mother's house. On these occasions he delivered speeches of great beauty but at the same time so full of ungodly ideas that Monica could not bear to listen to them.

When these meetings became more regular, Monica began to have her doubts about letting Augustine continue with this in her own house. It was just too difficult for her to hear ideas so directly against Christ's teachings proclaimed under her own roof. Pondering these things, she suddenly remembered that the Lord Jesus had said, "He who loves his son or daughter more than Me is not worthy of Me." Suddenly she knew exactly what to do, although it was very difficult to put into practice.

"Augustine," she said sternly, "we cannot go on like this."

"What do you mean Mother?"

"You know very well what I mean. I will no longer let you proclaim all these Manichaean ideas in my house. You shall have to stop it or. . . ."

Augustine laughed at her.

"Or what?" he asked.

"You shall have to leave this house!" she replied in earnest.

"I am a Manichaean, and I shall speak about it whenever I please," Augustine said haughtily.

"In that case, there is no longer room for you in this house," said Monica pointing a commanding finger toward the door.

"As you please," was the cool reply.

Augustine gathered his bags and books and walked into the street.

Inside, a sad and hurt Mother fell exhausted onto a chair. At that moment she was unable to pray, nor did she have any tears to express her sorrow.

This caused quite a turmoil among the people of Tagaste, who loved all sorts of scandals. Augustine, however, was far too proud to worry about that. "I have been shown the door," he said, "because the truth can no longer be freely spoken. It does not worry me though. I'm sure I can find another place to stay."

When he knocked on Mayor Romanianus' door,

he was made most welcome. He was treated with great generosity and enjoyed the splendid hospitality. The mayor had just purchased a villa in the country with hot baths and gaming facilities. He

was allowed to participate in all the amusements his host had to offer, which left him little time to make the speeches he used to hold in his mother's house. Many grand banquets were held in the mayor's villa. He loved to hear his friend Augustine talk about all kinds of topics, especially about

Manichaeism. In the end, he too was won for this religion, just like so many of Augustine's friends.

Meanwhile, the faithful Monica remained at home, crying many tears over her wayward son. She begged the Lord to tear him away from the evil teachings, and soon she began to feel regret at having sent Augustine away. She realized that living with the mayor would make things worse for her son rather than better. Oh why had she sent him away?

In the end, she went to see her bishop, an old and wise man, who knew God's Word well.

She asked him to go and speak to her son and to convince him that Manichaeism was nothing but a lie.

The old man shook his head.

"That would achieve nothing, Monica," he said. "Your son is so clever and can speak so fluently that he would just outtalk me. But you must never give up hope. Look at me. You know that I love the Lord sincerely, but in my youth I was also a Manichaean."

Monica's eyes were wide with surprise when she heard that, but she still persisted. "Could you at least try?"

"Believe me, it would do no good!" he assured her. "But you can also believe that a son who has been prayed for so much cannot be lost for God."

With that Monica departed, but she repeated the words over and over in her mind: "A son who has been prayed for so much cannot be lost for God!"

"Oh Lord, let that which Thy servant has spoken become true!" she prayed.

# CHAPTER SEVEN

## THE DEATH OF A FRIEND

In the middle of one of his lectures, Augustine received a message that one of his friends[3] was dying, and was asked to come.

Immediately Augustine left his students and hurried to the house of his dying friend. They had been friends for a long time. In Carthage they had lived together for a while, and when Augustine had become a Manichaean, he had talked his friend into becoming one as well. But now his friend was dying.

Augustine hurried on. He was convinced that he could make his friend feel better.

When Augustine arrived at the house, the young man was unable to speak. Shortly before, he had been baptized, and that had apparently tired him out.

At last Augustine was allowed to see the lad.

"What have they done with you?" he laughed. "Did you really have yourself baptized? Man, how could you do that?"

Augustine was sure that they had the young man baptized without his permission, out of superstition.

He soon found out differently.

The young man was very well aware of what had happened, as he had professed his faith before being baptized. He looked at Augustine with dark eyes and said, "I am very grateful for what happened, Augustine, and I feel very much at peace now."

---

[3] The name of this friend is not known. In his *Confessions* Augustine does not mention him.

Again Augustine laughed. "How is that possible? We were always such faithful followers of Mani, and now you go and do this. I cannot understand it at all!"

The dying young man tried to raise himself a little. He had always looked up to the clever Augustine, but now, with an unaccustomed boldness, he said, "Listen here Augustine, if you would like to remain my friend, you must stop this mocking and scorning!"

Augustine could feel himself becoming angry but was able to restrain himself.

He hoped that his friend would soon feel better. Then he would show him the error of his ways. He was sorry that he could not argue the point with him right now; it would simply have to wait until later.

"I'll come back and discuss it with you later," he said carelessly. "Make sure that you soon feel better."

The friend did not recover. He died a few days later without Augustine seeing him again.

The news about his friend's death came as a terrible blow to him. It disturbed him so much that on occasion he became quite unreasonable, and at night in bed he cried for hours.

He had fallen victim to despair, and he could no longer remain in Tagaste.

"I'm leaving," he told the mayor.

"But Augustine, what is wrong with you?" asked Romanianus. "I thought you enjoyed being here. Come on, tomorrow we will go hunting all day. That will soon make you feel better!"

Augustine sadly shook his head. "I have to go. I cannot stay here another day. I am going back to Carthage. There I shall open a school for public speaking and try to make a living that way."

"I think you are making a big mistake, but if I cannot persuade you to stay, I will help you get started. Licentius can go with you. Then at least you will have one student, and if you like, you may also take his brother along. That makes two of them."

"I'll be very grateful," said Augustine. For if the truth were told, he did not have that much confidence in the prospects of a new school.

Romanianus was a generous man. He not only gave Augustine money to pay for the trip but also some to tie him over the first difficult period.

The farewell to his mother was short. She had her fears about the big city with its many temptations. Did not that girl Lepida live there? She was not at all sure that Augustine was doing the right thing, so naturally she tried to change his mind. But she soon realized that that was impossible. All she said then was, "Go with God, Augustine. Your mother shall continue to pray for you."

Augustine laughed!

# CHAPTER EIGHT

## AUGUSTINE DECEIVES HIS MOTHER

One day, toward the evening, Monica and Augustine walked together to the port.

He had tried to convince his mother that he was going to say goodbye to a friend who was on his way to Rome, but Monica had the feeling that it was Augustine himself who was going to Rome.

"It would be better if you told me the truth, Augustine," she said. "You yourself are going to Rome!"

"What is so bad about that Mother?"

"Oh Augustine, the temptations in Rome are even greater than in Carthage. Don't you understand? Please stay in Africa. This is your country, and I would so love to have you near me."

"That is quite possible Mother, but I am going to Rome. At the moment, Alypius is studying law there, and he has written and told me so often to come to Rome also that I have decided to go. I shall be able to make a good living there, and the students in Rome are better behaved than in Carthage!"

"So your mind is made up?" asked Monica.

"Certainly, Mother. Honoratus and Marcianus have urged me to go. They told me I'd be a fool not to go!"

"Then I shall come with you, Augustine!"

"But Mother, what are you going to do in Rome?" asked the startled Augustine. He could not bear the thought of having his mother around every day.

She would interfere with everything and would not allow him to have parties with his friends. No, Mother was not to come along!

"Do you really have to ask what I would do in Rome? Why, care and pray for you of course!"

"You can do that in Tagaste just as well–praying, I mean," he said bluntly.

"I know that, but the Lord has given you to me. I must care for you, not only for your soul but for your body as well."

"All right then," was the indifferent reply.

They had come to the harbour where the ship was anchored. Monica thought that she could board right away, but Augustine told her that it would be quite a while before the ship would sail.

I'll try and find out a bit more," he said and quickly walked onto the ship. A few of his friends were already on board, and he told them about his mother's determination to come with him. They offered him some advice, and before long, Augustine was back with his mother, telling her that it might be as long as a few more hours before the ship could weigh anchor, as it had to wait for a favourable wind.

"Then we shall wait," Monica said, resigned. They walked up and down the quay in the evening light, and when Monica became tired she sat down on a stone bench.

After some time, when the signal for departure had still not been given, Augustine said that he would go and find out how things stood. He came back with the message that it could take the entire night before the ship would be able to leave the harbour.

Monica sighed. "Oh dear, what a pity. I am so tired, and the temperature won't go down, as there is not even a slight breeze to cool the night air. I am just about ready to faint."

"Really mother, it is too bad that you should sit here all night. There is a chapel nearby. Let us go there. You can sit down there and maybe even catch up on a little sleep."

That idea appealed to Monica. She was so very tired, and if the ship could not leave before tomorrow morning, she might as well rest in the chapel porch. Together they walked the short distance to the chapel, and soon Augustine had found his mother a comfortable place to sit down. They were not the only people there. Others had come to find a place to sleep, mostly the poor of the city but also a few travellers looking for a cool spot to spent the hot evening hours. It was impossible to talk much, but Monica did not mind. She had enough to do. She continuously prayed that the Lord would guard and keep her son and that He would turn him to faith in Christ the Saviour and make him His child. Gradually her eyes became heavy, and she began to doze off. After a while Augustine gently lowered her down to the floor, and she was soon asleep, as though she were at home in her own bed.

That was exactly what Augustine had been waiting for! He tiptoed out of the chapel and ran toward the ship. He was greeted with shouts of joy. "You fixed that beautifully, Augustine," his friends called. "Come on skipper, there's a breeze coming. Hoist the mainsail and let's go!"

Indeed, a breeze was coming in. The sails were hoisted, and slowly the vessel floated out of the harbour and into the Bay of Carthage. Augustine, leaning over the side, did not join in the boisterous fun his friends were having. The hot, sultry evening bothered him. He did not hear the shouts of the crew, either. He gazed towards the slowly vanishing coast of North Africa, his homeland. There in that small chapel lay his sleeping mother, or perhaps she had already woken up. Would she already have discovered the deceitful trick her son had played on her?

Augustine could feel his heart pound uneasily. What had his mother ever done to him that he dared treat her in such a terrible way? Had she not always been good to him?

Augustine's conscience began to plague him, and he accused himself of being a liar, a deceiver, a cheat.

However, this did not last very long.

He reassured himself by thinking that his mother should have had more sense. She should have realized that she would find it impossible to live in far-away Rome.

It was different for him. He had to go there to

earn a living. Actually, the trip to Rome was also a flight for Augustine. He was fleeing from Carthage, because there he was known as a Manichaean. He had begun to realize that his religion was a deceitful, human invention; however, he was still a Manichaean, and lately followers of this teaching had, especially in Numidia, become the object of a rather severe persecution. The emperor Theodosius would not tolerate Manichaeans among his subjects. Augustine suspected that in Carthage he would be in danger and had therefore decided to go to Rome. He was not known in that city, and as soon as he had saved enough money, he would also send for Lepida, with whom he had, against the wishes of his mother, an immoral relationship. She could then bring their young son Adeodatus with her to Rome.

Thus Augustine tried to quiet his conscience, but he did not feel at peace. Time and again the image of his faithful mother thwarted his endeavours to silence his conscience. How could he possibly have dared to treat his mother in this selfish, deceitful way?

When Monica awoke from her sleep, she looked around, puzzled, and mumbled "Augustine?" But Augustine was not there!

The friendly chapel gatekeeper came toward her. "Are you looking for someone, madam?" he asked. "I thought I heard you mention a name."

"I am looking for my son; he was here last night. We are leaving together by ship for Rome."

"Do you mean the *Aeolus*, madam?"

"Yes—yes, that is the name of the ship."

"But that ship is no longer in port, madam."

"What do you mean?"

"I mean that it sailed late last night."

"But what about my son?" she wanted to ask. But

she held the words back just in time. Her misery was no concern of the gatekeeper.

Outwardly calm, she said, "That is a pity. I thank you for the information."

She left the porch and walked towards the harbour. There were always people looking out over the ocean, and she asked an old skipper, "Has the *Aeolus* left?"

"Yes madam, last night already. She sailed at the first sign of a breeze. If you look carefully, you can see a little speck in the distance. That is her."

Monica strained to see the little speck, but soon her tears blurred everything in sight. She greeted the old skipper and staggered back to town, a broken woman.

Back in Tagaste, she was alone with her tears and her thoughts.

# CHAPTER NINE

## ROME:
## A BITTER DISAPPOINTMENT

No sooner had Augustine arrived in Rome and found lodgings with a fellow Manichaean, when he became seriously ill. Suffering from a very high fever, he was convinced that he would die. The thought of death terrified him, and no wonder. He lived a life far from God, and no one living far from the Lord can face death with peace in his heart.

However, he was nursed excellently, and after a while he began to recover. He had not believed that he would ever get better. It would be a long time before he realized that his mother's prayers had played an important role in his recovery.

Now that he was better, he had to get to work. He set out to find students, and to do that he had to make many visits to parents. He was received with cordiality everywhere. On top of that, the autumn rains had begun, and the mornings and evenings were rather chilly. Augustine, who had a weak chest, was used to the warm climate of Northern Africa, and the cold really bothered him.

All in all, Rome was a big disappointment, and he was now sorry that he had ever wanted to exchange Carthage for the "eternal" city. Its steep hills tired him considerably, and the sharp stones on the roads caused his feet pain.

Each evening, after having spent the day walking through Rome, he was exhausted when he reached his lodgings.

The house was located in a rather unpleasant

neighbourhood, full of dubious Eastern characters: Greeks, Syrians, Egyptians, and Armenians.

When at last he reached his attic room after climbing six flights of stairs, he sat down, teeth chattering with cold, in front of his little heater with its smoky, glowing charcoal. The only light available was the tiny flame from a small oil lamp.

Augustine hated Rome!

Never in his life had things gone so badly for him as here in this famous city.

All this, after having such high expectations of the place. Also, strangers were not really welcome in Rome. Only a few years before, all strangers, including professors, had been banned from Rome as unproductive consumers because the city had feared a shortage of food.

Fortunately he found his friend Alypius, who set out to find him the students he so badly needed. Alypius himself had been given a job with the imperial administration and was now advisor to the treasurer-general. Yes, Alypius had been very fortunate indeed, and like a good friend, he made sure that Augustine obtained work. Before long, he had quite a few students to teach.

Augustine started teaching. In his free time he and his friend enjoyed much public entertainment, although he never went to the gladiator sword fights because he could not stand the sight of blood. One day Alypius did go to the fights; his friends almost dragged him there. So Alypius did go, but he decided to close his eyes for the duration of the fights and sit with his head down.

Suddenly he heard an enormous shout. The crowd was wildly screaming as the first victim fell, wounded, to the ground. At that sound, Alypius automatically opened his eyes and saw blood oozing from the victim. As soon as he saw that, he became obsessed with the cruel game and returned to the arena to see the fights as often as he could. Augustine tried to keep him away, but that was far from easy.

In the meantime, Augustine experienced many strange things with his fellow Manichaeans. First, there was Bishop Faustus whom, while Augustine was living in Carthage, he had held in high esteem. This man taught moderation but indulged in food to such an extend that it often made him sick. Then there was the case of another Manichaean

bishop that was even worse. He was caught stealing the church funds.

All these things caused Augustine to doubt the whole Manichaean religion. Yet he remained one of them, but only because they might one day be useful to him. And indeed they would, which soon became evident.

After he had taught his students for a considerable time, he told them in a roundabout way that it was time they paid him some money. After all, he had to live also! He was still the guest of a fellow Manichaean, but it went against Augustine's nature to be continually beholden to the man, unable to pay a cent in return. So the students would have to pay something.

The next day, not one student turned up. They had decided that if they had to pay, they might as well go to another teacher.

So all at once Augustine was without a job and without money.

Miserably, he went to see his friend Alypius.

"What am I to do?" he asked. "I am stranded without a cent to my name. Oh, if only I had the money to go back to Carthage!"

"Don't be too hasty," laughed Alypius. "We will try something else first."

"What is that?" asked Augustine in anticipation.

"Look here, the government of Milan is looking for a lecturer in rhetoric (public speaking), precisely your subject. If you could get that position, all your troubles would be over; you would have a good, steady income!"

Augustine became excited.

That was exactly what he needed. He would no longer be dependent on his students. It would not even matter whether he had many or only a few students.

"How can I possibly get that job?" he asked.

"That will not be easy. They are holding a competition, and the one who sends in the best answer will get the job, if he has someone to recommend him."

"That takes care of my chances," said Augustine.

"I don't know a soul in Milan. Who on earth could recommend me?"

"Well, Mr. Symmoctus, the prefect of Milan, that is who!"

"Come on, that is impossible."

"That is possible," continued Alypius. "You are a Manichaean, are you not?"

"Well, yes, sort of; but I must confess that it no longer means much to me."

"That is all right, as long as you are still one of them. You are, aren't you?"

"Certainly I am."

"Well then, let your landlord write to Symmoctus. He is a fanatic follower of Manichaeus, and he will decide the winner of the competition. If I were you, I would get it underway immediately. You may be lucky. And as far as your landlord is concerned, I shall have a talk with him myself."

As soon as he got home, Augustine started working on the competition question, and his friends in Rome sent a warm recommendation to Symmoctus. The result was the prefect of Milan appointed Augustine as lecturer of rhetoric. Now he had a secure job and a steady income.

Augustine was elated!

# CHAPTER TEN

## AUGUSTINE IN MILAN

A ship was sailing on the Mediterranean. It had come from Carthage and was now on its way to Ostia, the entrance port to Rome.

On board was a fifty-four-year-old woman. It was Monica, Augustine's mother. Her son had written to her from Milan and told her that he was now a professor with a steady income. He had written, "With a carriage of the imperial service, I rode from Rome to Milan like a king! "

No sooner had Monica read the letter then she decided that she too would go to Milan. She would leave Africa to be with her son. The well-loved Bishop Ambrosius lived in Milan, and maybe Augustine would come to repentance there.

Monica made a big sacrifice when she decided to go to Milan. The property she owned in her beloved Tagaste allowed her a comfortable living.

However, she gladly made that sacrifice to be with her son. She knew that she would find it hard to live in a place where no one knew her, but nothing could stop her from going.

The sea voyage was not easy, and it was made worse when they were hit with heavy gale's. Monica sat on the aft deck with the other travellers, most of them paralyzed with fear. Suddenly Monica threw back her widow's veil, jumping up as though she personally wanted to fight the enormous waves, and with colour coming into her white face, she said to the sailors, "What are you afraid of? We shall all arrive safely. I am sure of it!" When the sailors laughed at the woman who knew nothing whatsoever about bringing a ship across the ocean, she said solemnly, "God has assured me of our safe arrival!"

That silenced the sailors, who now put more effort into their work than before.

Monica was proven right. The ship did arrive safely in Ostia. The journey over land from Rome to Milan was equally difficult. Rough transport over an even rougher road. No imperial carriage for Monica!

Miserable with fatigue, Monica reached Milan, but all the difficulties were forgotten the moment she embraced her son. She was reunited with Augustine. Surely, all would be well now.

Monica was faced with a busy life. Augustine had rented a few rooms, but because the owner himself did not live in the house, he was allowed the use of the entire property. That was very good of the owner but now the house also had to be put to good use. That posed no great problem. The custom in those days was that if someone had a large house, his relations expected to be given a home there also. That is what happened in this case too. When Monica arrived, she found Lepida, the girl from Carthage with Adeodatus, Augustine and Lepida's son. Then there was Navigius, Augustine's brother, and also his cousins Rusticus and Lastidianus.

Alypius had also taken up residence at his friend's house together with Netridius, an acquaintance from Carthage. That was quite a gathering and a rather large responsibility for Monica to make sure that they lived satisfactorily. Lepida was not much help in this either. She came from a very poor family, and when Augustine began to think of really marrying her, his mother advised him against it. She convinced Lepida that she did not actually fit into their kind of environment, and the girl agreed with her. She definitely did not feel at ease with these learned people. She decided not to stand in the way of Augustine's aspirations to greatness and fame, and so she went back to Africa. She really loved Augustine, so much that she never married anyone else.

It goes without saying that Monica, from the first day on, went to the church where Bishop[4] Ambrosius preached.

"What do you think of this Ambrosius, Mother?" asked Augustine.

"He explains God's Word in the most beautiful way. During each sermon I keep thinking, 'I wish Augustine could hear this. Then maybe he would find peace.' Why don't you come with me sometime?"   Augustine laughed. "Why would I do that, Mother? I don't believe a thing he says."

"But Son, He brings us the Word of God, the Gospel, The glad tidings of salvation and deliverance for lost sinners."

"I am glad you appreciate it, Mother, but it does nothing for me. When I came first to Milan, I paid him a courtesy visit, but he treated me rather haughtily."

"Don't you understand why?"

"No, why should I?"

"You were appointed by Symmoctus, who is a Manichaean and the fiercest opponent of Ambrosius. If that man is your benefactor, it is no wonder that the bishop does not trust you."

"Do you really think that is the case, Mother? Well, he is probably right, but is he a good speaker?"

---

[4] What we today call a minister the ancient church used to call bishop meaning overseer.

"He is a great orator."

"Good, then I'll come and listen one day. Just to see how he says things. What he says does not interest me."

"But Augustine, how can you say such a thing?" asked Monica.

However, he did go with his mother to hear the bishop speak, not just once, but several times. On these occasions Monica would ask the Lord to bless the words he heard in church, so that he too would learn to love the Saviour. These prayers were not answered for a long time, yet something in Augustine began to change. Gradually he also began to listen to what Ambrosius said and the wisdom the bishop drew from the Holy Scriptures amazed him.

Some of his sermons made a great impression on Augustine, and when he began to ponder them, he found himself to be in a lamentable state. He was a professor, a very learned one, he earned a good salary, he had his mother and his friends around him every day, he had a lovely house with a big garden, but none of these things satisfied him, nor did they bring him inner peace. The unrest in his heart remained. He was insecure, and the thought of death terrified him.

On Christmas day, Ambrosius preached on John 1:1—"In the beginning was the Word, and the Word was with God and the Word was God."

Augustine was very excited about that sermon, and he talked about it for days. Even his mother could feel hope dawning in her heart.

# CHAPTER ELEVEN

# UNDER THE FIG TREE

One afternoon when Augustine and his friend Alypius were home together, a visitor was announced. It was Pontitianus, a high official from the imperial court. He was, like Augustine, originally from Africa, and he had come to meet his learned fellow countryman. They made themselves comfortable, and during the conversation, a few Epistles of Paul, on the table in front of him, caught the eye of the visitor.

Pontitianus, who was a Christian, immediately began to talk about them. As they talked, Pontitianus told Augustine and Alypius that a short while ago he and two other courtiers had visited Trieste. While wandering around the countryside the two courtiers had come upon a hut where two poor hermits lived. The hermits were reading a book about the life of their great leader Antonius. The visitors asked to read it also, and when they did they were greatly affected by the faith of Antonius, so much that they decided then and there to give up their position at the court to join the hermits and lead pious lives. It had been a great sacrifice, because both men were engaged to be married.

After Pontitianus had left, a great restlessness settled on Augustine. He envied the courtiers who had unexpectedly found real peace.

Suddenly, he grabbed Alypius by the arm and began to shake him.

"Tell me!" he shouted. "Did you hear that story? What do you think of it? Don't you think it was ridiculous? Simple people can claim heaven while we learned people, full of knowledge, stand on the side and watch?"

His voice was strangely hoarse. Alypius looked at his friend in surprise. He saw that his face had undergone a complete change. It seemed as if heaven had suddenly come very close to Augustine and he was filled with a consuming desire to be part of it.

Augustine ran into the garden and fell down on a bench. He was found there by Alypius, who had started to worry about his friend. Augustine never noticed that his friend sat down next to him. He was fighting an inner battle. His entire ungodly life displayed itself before his eyes. He wanted to free himself from his sins, but he could not.

Suddenly, he got up from the bench and ran further into the garden. In the farthest corner under a fig tree he fell to his face,and panting, full of hesitation, Augustine uttered his first real prayer: "How long? Oh, how long? Tomorrow? Always tomorrow, why not right away? Why can I not put a stop to this sinful life right away?"

But listen—what was that? The garden next door was separated from him by a wall, and from behind that wall came the voice of a girl singing, "Tolle, lege," which meant "Take, read!"

Augustine did not know the song. He had never heard it. The words were completely new to him. So he believed they were sent by God as a direct message to him.

"Take,read! That is a command from God," he thought.

He jumped up from the ground and went to the bench where Alypius was still waiting for him. There were the Epistles of Paul, which Alypius had taken with him into the garden. Augustine picked them up, and the first words he read hit him like lightning. He read, "But put on the Lord Jesus Christ, and make no provisions for the flesh to gratify its desires."

"Alypius," he said, "listen to this. These words are for me. God has sent them to me straight from heaven." His face glowed with happiness while he spoke. The restlessness had left his eyes, and a great peace had settled in his heart. He closed the book.

But Alypius calmly said, "I am very glad about that, Augustine, and your mother certainly will be even more. But you also have to read what follows."

Again Augustine opened the book and read, "As for the man who is weak in faith, welcome him, but not for disputes over opinions."

"Don't you think that these words are also written for you, Augustine?"

"Oh yes, these words are certainly for me!" answered his friend. "I can feel it, Alypius. My newfound faith is still very weak. My pride could still stand in its way. I want to become a Christian; I want it with all my heart, but now I still have to become one!"

Alypius nodded his head. It was exactly as Augustine said.

"Now I must go to Mother" he said.

The professor ran toward the house. Alypius let him go. He realized only too well that this meeting between mother and son allowed no room for a third party.

Coming into the house, Augustine went straight to Monica's room. He ran toward her, and with the words, "Oh Mother, the Lord has delivered me," he fell into her arms.

"My boy, my boy!" She sobbed, "then we can now travel the same road together!"

With that she burst into tears.

"Lord, I thank Thee for allowing me to see this day."

That night Monica did not sleep. She could not! Now, however it was not with sorrow as on so many other nights. But she was too joyful to settle down to sleep.

At last the Lord had heard her prayers. Now her task on earth was finished. All she wanted to do was sing His praises and go in peace.

# CHAPTER TWELVE

# A WINTER IN CASSICIACUM

Only three weeks until the annual holidays! Augustine was really looking forward to them. He suffered from chronic bronchitis, due to the damp climate, and he needed a good rest. However, that was not all. After his conversion, Augustine wanted to spend his entire life in the service of the Lord. He wanted to leave his post as professor of oratory. His poor health provided him with a good excuse to ask for his release, because he did not want his conversion to cause a fuss.

That is what a certain Victorinus had done earlier, but it went against Augustine's nature. Calmly, although with difficulty, he completed his work, and when the three weeks were up, he resigned as professor of oratory.

Then he faced the question of what to do now? It stood to reason that no job meant no money. It was indeed a difficult situation.

Again Romanianus, the generous mayor of Tagaste, came to the rescue. He also lived in Milan because his son Licentius attended Augustine's lectures there.

He suggested that Augustine continue to teach Licentius. The mayor would pay him a handsome wage, and when another student, Trygelius, asked him the same favor, the question was settled. Augustine would make a living as a private tutor.

Now all that remained was the problem of accommodation. His health did not allow him to spend his vacation in Milan. It was just too damp. A certain professor, Verecundus, solved that problem for him. Augustine had once done him a favour, and the man wanted to do something in return.

"Friend," he said to Augustine, "I own a villa named Cassiciacum, a long way outside Milan. If you like you may spend your vacation there. You'll soon find out that the climate there is very healthy!"

"Naturally, I would love to go, but, ah . . . ."

"Say no more! I know what you mean. Your finances are rather low, and now you are worried about the rent. Well, let me assure you that you can live there free of charge!"

"But Verecundus, are you sure?"

"Of course I am sure. There is only one condition, and that is that you care for the property and look after it as best you can.
Is that agreeable?"

"Absolutely, but . . . ah . . . my mother."

"Man stop worrying! The house is large and roomy. Take your mother with you. Take anyone else you want to take. You can go there with your entire family!"

Augustine was elated. Verecundus was a good and loyal friend!

As soon as possible, they shifted to the villa. It sported many rooms, several bathrooms, spacious hall, and a large dining room. It was surrounded by farmland and large meadows.

A row of chestnut trees protected the house from the glaring sun. Peace and quiet reigned everywhere, and the air was so pure that Augustine's diseased chest immediately began to feel better.

The first night, going to bed in Cassiciacum, Augustine knelt down and prayed for Verecundus, "Thou, O Lord, wilt reward him on the day of resurrection. Thou who art faithful to Thy promises give Verecundus, for the use of this villa where we can rest from our worldly cares, the riches of an everlasting paradise."

Mother Monica again took on the care of the household. That certainly was a big job, as there were seven people to care for. The rest of the work was divided equally among the occupants. Alypius, who had also come along with them, had a good head for business. He kept all the books and did all the buying and selling.

Nearly every day he went into Milan to organize these things. Augustine himself took care that the day labourers who worked the land did their work and received their pay. The young people who were there were kept busy studying. The only problem Augustine had was Licentius,the mayor's son from Tagaste. He  was a truly spoiled child. Yet he was the darling of the household. He was lively, excitable, cheeky, and rather proud.

He was also rather impertinent, and if given the chance, would even play tricks on his teacher. Sometimes he was in such a bad mood that he would argue with everyone. But although he was a difficult boy, he had a soft heart. He was also rather a glutton and loved drinking, but Monica would have none of that. She kept a sober table.

Licentius could write beautiful poetry, and Augustine wrote to his father that he was nearly a perfect poet.

One day after dinner, Monica suddenly heard a loud voice singing, "God of hosts restore us now. Upon us cause Thy face to shine, and save us Lord for we are Thine!" It was a new song that was often sung in church.

"Augustine, who could be singing psalms that loud?" Monica asked.

Augustine had no idea, and at his mother's request, he went to find out. The sound came from somewhere outside.

After a while Augustine returned, accompanied by Licentius. "Here is the culprit! He was sitting on the privy[5] singing this beautiful psalm over and over again, more than ten times."

Licentius stood there, smiling, but Monica could not see the funny side of it at all.

"You ought to be ashamed Licentius," she said. "That is not a place to sing a beautiful psalm."

She lectured him severely on the subject. Licentius, however, had his answer ready. "Just imagine, little mother," he said,"if an enemy had locked me in there. Do you mean to say that God would not have heard me there?" Monica did not know what to say. The next day when Augustine spoke to him about it, he appeared to have forgotten all about it. He was not sorry at all for what he had done.

The winter soon passed, along with all the work that had to be done. Between lessons Augustine found time to write a few books, and he was also busy preparing himself for the baptism he would receive at Easter.

At last the long-awaited day dawned! April 25, 387. The simple service took place Easter night. The many candles burning in their holders gave the big church in Milan a sedately happy atmosphere. The Christians of Milan had all come together, although Easter did not start before the first light came. During Easter night, according to tradition, those catechumens who had prepared themselves received baptism. There was a reverent silence in the church. Monica had also come. That

---

5 Today we call this a toilet.

day she experienced the happiest hour of her life. She had grown old, but her eyes shone with grateful joy. The psalms that were sung created a beautiful sound under the high dome of the church. The baptismal service during the Easter night always drew a large congregation, but this one was even more special because the famous professor of oratory would receive baptism.

The voice of Ambrosius could be heard, "Aurelius Augustinus, I baptize you in the name of the Father and of the Son and of the Holy Spirit."

Suddenly the congregation sang the "Te Deum" ("Thee God"):

*We praise Thee, Lord our God,*
*We magnify Thy Name.*
*That every creature here*
*Thy splendour may proclaim!*
*Sing, choirs of angels, sing*
*His mighty works and wonder.*
*Uninterrupted be*
*Your Hallelujah yonder!*
*Yes, Thou art three times holy,*
*Lord of our salvation,*
*May earth and heaven be*
*Thy glory's revelation!*

Softly, Monica joined in the singing, and at the same time she whispered, "This, my son was dead, but now he lives. All thanks and praise be to God."

# CHAPTER THIRTEEN

# MONICA GOES HOME

Licentius had brought an alarming message when he returned from Milan. The country was under threat of war. It was Maxentius who wanted to attack Italy, and his first target was to be Milan. That message settled their deliberations.

After his own baptism and his son's, Augustine asked his mother if she would like to go back to Africa. Monica replied that she would like nothing better. After all, she still owned a house and land in Tagaste, and if Augustine would go with her, she could think of nothing she would rather do.

Back to her own country! Back home, as she would say. Augustine also wanted to go back there. Now that he had put his ungodly life behind him, the things he liked doing most were thinking, speaking, and writing about his Saviour and about serving Him. He wanted to defend Christianity against all who would attack it with different heresies.

At a family conference, all proved to be in favour of leaving Cassiciacum. That summer big plans were made for the coming journey, but they were not put into action with any great speed. It was, of course, no little matter to move from Milan to Tagaste, especially not in those days. No wonder, then, that the plans remained at the talking stage.

Then suddenly Licentius had come in with his bombshell message, and right away a decision was reached. Before the week was out, the entire family was on its way to Ostia, the port of Rome.

It proved to be a difficult journey, more so because it was midsummer.

They had not left a day too soon, for already in August the conqueror took his troops across the Alps and quickly advanced towards Milan. The young emperor Valentinianus fled with his court to Aqualegea. Augustine was very glad that he and his family had left Cassiciacum just in time.

Meanwhile, the journey to Ostia had become very grueling, and Monica, who was now fifty-six years old was very weak when they finally arrived at port.

Naturally, there was no ship waiting for them. They simply had to wait for suitable transport, and even when that was available, the weather was often far too rough to attempt the crossing.

Monica and Augustine had been privileged to find accommodation with Christian friends, so they did not have to depend on the noisy overcrowded inns of the port city.

Monica and her son did a lot of talking in those days of waiting. Sometimes at night they sat next to each other by the open window, admiring the myriads of stars in the firmament.

"We marvel at the greatness of Thy works, oh my God!" Augustine would later write in his book *Confessions*.

Beyond the hills lay the city of Rome with her palaces and her temples, with her gilt and marble.

One evening, when they again sat together admiring the stars and prayerfully acknowledging God's might, Monica said to Augustine, "Are you sure we are going home, Augustine?"

"Certainly we are, Mother. As soon as there is a ship available we shall go back to Tagaste."

"Yes . . . yes . . . I know that, but would you

believe that I would much rather go to the home of my Father in heaven?"

"But Mother! You are still young. We can yet have a long and happy time together!"

"No my son, believe me, my time has come. There was only one thing for which I wanted to live, and that was the day that you might come to believe in the Lord. God has granted me this great blessing.

You love the Saviour and not only have become a Christian, but you also want to spend your life in His service. You want to write in defense of His Church. Oh Augustine, I am so happy, and now I begin to wonder what I am waiting for here on earth. I sincerely hope that the Lord will take me to Himself. Only then will I truly have come home."

"You should not be so gloomy Mother. You probably feel like that because you are tired. In the morning, when you have had a good night's sleep, you will feel different."

But things did not change.

Before the week was out, Monica became ill. A severe fever wracked her body, and she felt a weariness come over her. She had to stay in bed and soon lost consciousness.

Everyone was standing around her bed, Augustine and his brother Navigius and also little Adeodatus. Then there were Rusticus and Lastidianus, two cousins from Tagaste, and a friend, Evodius. They all knew that mother Monica was dying.

Monica trembled. She sat up straight, and staring at all those around her, she asked, "Where am I?"

She saw the sad faces looking at her and understood that she would die.

She whispered to Augustine, "You had better bury me in Ostia."

These words came as a terrible shock to Navigius. Did Mother really mean that she would die? But she couldn't! He sobbed, "No! No, dear Mother! You will soon feel better! You cannot die here in a strange land. Wait until you have gone back to your own country!"

Monica looked at him and asked Augustine, "Did you hear what he said?"

Augustine nodded. He wholeheartedly agreed with his brother. After a while, Monica said, "Don't worry about me. You may bury me where you like. On the day of resurrection the Lord will find me no matter where I am."

In Tagaste she owned a family vault in which Patricius had been laid to rest, and she had always hoped that she would be put beside him. But now, suddenly, she seemed free from that desire.

Monica's life dragged on for a few more days. Then on the ninth day of her illness, she breathed her last. Augustine closed his mother's eyes. Mother Monica had gone home.

A sudden loud cry rent the silence in the room. It was Adeodatus. The little boy had been so moved by his grandmother's death that no one could quiet him. In the end, someone had to take him outside the room. Evodius took the book of Psalms and began to sing, "Oh Lord, I shall sing of Thy mercy, and Thy righteousness I will praise." Everyone present joined in. It was as though each one of them had lost a mother.

Augustine was overcome with grief. With great sadness he recalled the misery he had caused his dear mother to suffer by his ungodly life.

According to her wishes, Monica was buried in Ostia. During the funeral Augustine was able to contain himself, but as soon as they returned home he became so grief stricken that he could hardly breathe. After taking a hot bath, he fell into a deep sleep of exhaustion.

The next day, when the memory of his dear, departed mother again became too much for him, he fell on his bed, sobbing. Then at last he cried bitter tears over the loss of his beloved mother, tears he had held back for a long time.

A few days later, things were easier for Augustine, and in the evening he was heard singing Ambrosius's evensong:

*Oh Lord, Creator of us all*
*Thou Ruler of the heavens, Who*
*Endows the day with sparkling light*
*And with sweet slumber robes the night*
*When bodies rest from anxious toil,*
*Regaining strength to till the soil.*
*From weary souls Thou takest grief.*
*From anguish doest Thou grant relief.*

Monica died in the late summer of 387. The autumn winds could start any day, and no one was prepared to undertake the now dangerous journey across the Mediterranean.

Added to that was the fact that the fleet of Maxentius now sailed the waters of the Mediterranean and more or less blocked the entrance into Africa. It was therefore a real possibility that by crossing, they might fall into the hands of the enemy.

All this was sufficient reason for Augustine to postpone his return to Tagaste until the next year. However, he did not remain in the noisy port city but instead settled in Rome. He spent his spare time acquainting himself with the actions of the Manichaeans, who had once been his brothers but were now his declared enemies.

He set out to obtain all kinds of proof of their latest exploits so that he could campaign against them. He also carefully studied their teachings so that he could better prove them to be wrong.

He visited several monasteries in the region. He was thinking of opening a monastery near Tagaste to spent his life there in peace and solitude. Little did he know that the Lord had completely different plans for him.

After having spent a year doing all these things, the time had come for him to return to Africa. In August 388 he made the trip from Ostia to Carthage. It was exactly four years since he had fled from his mother and landed in Ostia.

The sea was unusually calm and beautiful, making this a wonderful journey. All too soon the ship dropped anchor in the harbour of Carthage. An elder of the church, a certain Elogius, had come to the ship to greet Augustine. After that, he and all

those who had come with him were taken to the home of his friend, the lawyer Innocentius.

Augustine did not remain in Carthage for very long. His heart was drawn to Tagaste, where he had spent his youth as a farmer's son. Before much longer, he set out for the place of his birth. At last, Augustine had come home.

## CHAPTER FOURTEEN

# BISHOP OF HIPPO

Puzzled, the people looked at each other. "Have you heard? Augustine is back in Tagaste!"

"What? That boy of Patricius and Monica? I wonder what we have to put up with now!"

The people who spoke were in for a surprise. From the first Sunday on, Augustine attended the church services and listened attentively to the sermons.

In the weeks that followed, he did something that would endear him forever to the citizens of his hometown. He gave the little money that was left over from Patricius' estate to the poor. He gave the house and land that belonged to his parents to the church with the proviso that its usufruct[6] would be his for as long as he lived. After all, he had to have an income and a place to stay. Doing a thing like that was not unusual in those days. It provided an escape from hefty taxes, and because church property was inalienable[7], robbers were not feared.

---

6 Usufruct means to have the use of and the profit from something.

7 Inalienable means ownership can never be transferred to someone else.

When all this was settled, Augustine, with his son, his brother, and his friends Alypius and Evidius, went to live in his old parental home. Augustine's arrival was a much talked of subject in Tagaste. Many remembered the pious Monica, and they rejoiced in the fact that the ungodly young boy had become a God-fearing man.

Yet many wondered what this God-fearing man wanted to do in Tagaste.

Before long they would find out.

Augustine and his friends wanted to live in peace and solitude so that they could study God's Word, talk about it and above all, write about it! Augustine wanted to write commentaries on the various books of the Bible. It was going to be wonderful! Every morning when he saw the sun pour her golden rays over the beautiful forest behind his house, he would pray to God with all his heart, "My God, grant me the grace to live here under the shade of Thy peace while waiting for Thy glorious Paradise!"

He would then set to work. Book after book flowed from his pen. Some were about music, but he mostly wrote to combat false doctrines and keep the teachings of the church pure.

During this wonderful period in his life, Augustine suffered a great loss. His son, the very intelligent Adeodatus from whom Augustine had expected so much, became ill and died. That was a heavy blow for Augustine, but he bore it with true Christian fortitude. A few years later he would write in his book *Confessions*, "Thou didst take him from this earth after only a short time, but my heart is at peace when I think of him."

After a while, the Christians in Tagaste began to think it a shame that a learned man like Augustine sat at home, doing nothing but study and write.

Was he to hide his light under a bushel? Certainly not! Why was he not made an elder? Why did he not preach? He was certainly able to do so!

When Augustine found out what the people thought, he became afraid that they would assign him a task in the congregation. He was quite determined to continue living a quiet, isolated life. He had spent three wonderful years in Tagaste. Why did they want to put a stop to that? Well, he would soon fix that problem. Suddenly, Augustine moved to Hippo! Its real name was Hippo Regius, and it was a very important port. Today it is called Bone.

There in Hippo Augustine knew he would be left in peace. The congregation had its own bishop, Valerius. No, in Hippo there was no danger of being put to work.

That is how Augustine arrived in Hippo. Naturally he thought that he had gone there because he had wanted to, but actually it was the Lord who had brought him to that city.

Every Sunday Augustine would go to church and stand, listening to Valerius' sermons.

Yes, stand! In those days churches had neither pews nor chairs and the people stood for the duration of the service.

At first, things in Hippo went as Augustine had hoped. He was left alone. Then suddenly objections were voiced. Valerius was getting old, and besides that, he was a Greek whose knowledge of Latin was not very good, while he did not understand Punic, the common language, at all. The congregation had an even greater problem. Old Valerius had great difficulties dealing with troublemakers, and many times the people said, "We really need a young man to tackle these Donatists!"

In his sermon the following Sunday, Valerius

complained that he did not have enough helpers. There was a dire need for good elders. Standing among the faithful, Augustine heard the complaint. In his heart he had to agree with Valerius, but at the same time he was glad that no one knew he was in Hippo.

How wrong he was! People from Tagaste occasionally visited Hippo and would enquire after Augustine, so he certainly was no stranger in that congregation! He soon realized that the people knew about him only too well! Before Valerius could finish his sermon, some hotheads among the people had pushed their way toward Augustine.

Unexpectedly, they took him by the arms and led him toward the pulpit, shouting, "Make Augustine an elder! Make Augustine an elder!" Yes, that is the way things were done in those days. The same thing had happened to Ambrosius in Milan. If Augustine had dared to disagree, it could possibly have cost him his life. Therefore, Valerius quickly agreed before the meeting turned into a riot.

Augustine, believing that it was God's will, bowed to the call of the people. He told them he was willing to become an elder. But the thought of all the hardships he would now have to face, together with the realization that he would no longer be able to spend much time in his beloved study, brought tears to his eyes.

One of the people, seeing his tears, misunderstood them completely and said in a friendly manner, "You are right, you know! Being an elder is not good enough for you. You can be sure that one day you shall be our bishop!"

What was meant as a comforting remark actually made things worse.

Although he had agreed to the office of elder, he asked to have his ordination postponed until Easter. He felt the need to prepare himself for the task. Everyone agreed, but after he had been ordained at Easter, he realized that while an elder, he was doing the work of an assistant bishop. The old bishop soon left most of the work to Augustine. He had to preach, visit the sick, teach catechism classes, and even baptize. Augustine had become very busy, indeed. There was very little time left for talks with his friends. He really wanted those talks and decided to have these discussions during meals. Most of the time meals were spent in small talk that ended in abuse and gossip. On entering the dining room one day, Augustine's friends found a sheet of paper with the following rhyme on it attached to the wall:

*"Abusive speech and slanderous word,*
*Shall at this table not be heard."*

From then on, only constructive discussions accompanied each meal.

Meanwhile, Valerius had become aware that some of the neighbouring churches had their eye on Augustine. They wanted to appoint him bishop of their congregation.

One day the old bishop came to warn his elder Augustine to keep a low profile for the time being. Otherwise, he might be kidnapped and taken to a town to be made bishop of its congregation. The old man could not bear the thought of losing Augustine.

Augustine laughed at this.

"But my lord bishop, do you think I could do anything else but agree if that were God's will?"

"No . . . no . . . of course not. But oh, I would lose you. What would I do then?" Then suddenly, his eyes bright, he shouted, "I've got it. Yes! That is the solution! I shall appoint you assistant bishop of Hippo!"

"But you can't do that on your own, can you?"

"I won't! Bishop Aurelius of Carthage has a lot of influence. I shall have a word with him."

Aurelius agreed with the idea. After Valerius had gained the approval of the congregation, he was to call a convocation of bishops.

Naturally, the congregation wholeheartedly approved. When the convocation of bishops had come together, Valerius told them that the congregation would very much like to have Augustine appointed assistant bishop of Hippo, if the brothers agreed.

Only the old bishop of Guelua, Megalius, had objections. He deemed the whole idea unacceptable to the church. He brought up various things from Augustine's past life and said that he could not accept someone as bishop who had come to the Christian Church from the Manichaeans. People like that should not serve in an office of the church.

Nothing he said changed anyone's mind, and Augustine was made assistant bishop of Hippo. When Valerius died, Augustine was made bishop in his place and remained in that office until he too died.

It is difficult to realize just how much work Augustine did while serving the church of Hippo. Apart from the work any minister does, like preaching, teaching catechism classes, visiting families, the aged, the sick, and the troubled, he did a great deal more. For example, he wrote many, many letters to various people in his own country and abroad. These people all asked his advice on many different questions. He also wrote continually against heretics, especially the heretic Pelagius. This man had come from Ireland and proclaimed a doctrine completely against the Bible. Augustine realized this, and he never stopped warning the people not to listen to Pelagius. He attacked him in many various writings. It was Augustine who, by the grace of the Lord and with His help, kept the Christian Church from one of the most dangerous heresies.

The bishop of Hippo became one of the great Church Fathers.

This gallant knight of God used his wisdom and his love to fight for His Church. He attacked all heresies with Scripture itself and never ceased to proclaim the greatest truth: only the sacrifice of Christ's suffering and death can obtain man's salvation. He cannot ever earn even a small part of that by himself—not by much praying, not by good works, and certainly not through the intercession of the saints.

Already in those days there were people who prayed to the saints, but Augustine faithfully fought

against this practice. In one of his sermons he said,
"The holy martyrs receive an exalted place.

Their names are mentioned with reverence before
those of the other dead. However, they shall never
take the place of Christ in our prayers. That is not
done! It is not allowed!"

# CHAPTER FIFTEEN

# AUGUSTINE AND THE LITTLE BOY

A legend about Augustine tells us that he spent hours thinking about the question, "Who is God?"

It was impossible to find a satisfactory answer. He knew the teachings of the Bible about the highest knowledge of God being kept hidden from the wise and given to the children, but that did not stop him from trying to find the answer to this mystery. Time and again he asked himself, "Who is God?"

God has no beginning nor will He ever have an end. The last part was not too difficult, he thought, but the idea that God had no beginning, that God has always existed—who could ever understand that? "Even if I go back a million centuries," thought the bishop, "I will still find a point where these centuries started. Yet God existed before time began. No matter how far back I go, everywhere and always there will be God, He who has been forever. "The very thought of that made Augustine dizzy. He tried to use his great mind to understand this but found it impossible. He could not accept this and he hoped that he would see the day when he could comprehend this limitless time and space and clearly visualize it.

Once when he had again spent hours thinking about this, he put on his robe, and still deep in thought, went outside and walked toward the beach. The sandy stretch of shoreline was deserted. Augustine saw no one and nothing except the ever returning waves crashing upon the sand. When he reached the water line, he saw the seemingly unending body of water.

"Ah," he cried, "this is an image of the space in which my searching mind wanders and repeatedly gets lost. My spirit floats across the immeasurable surface of which it can see neither beginning nor end. Yet soon the bird returns to its nest as I must go home, weary with fatigue from thinking but never clearly understanding who and what God is!"

As he walked there, talking to himself, he saw a little boy playing in the sand, and he wondered what the child was doing there without anyone looking after him.

Wanting to find out, Augustine walked to where the boy sat on the sand. As he came closer, he saw that the child was very handsome indeed. With his hands the boy had dug a hole in the sand and was now busy filling it with water from the sea.

Augustine kindly asked the lad, "What are you doing my boy? You seem so busy!"

"Please do not bother me," said the child. "I have dug a hole and now I am going to put the whole ocean into it."

That made Augustine laugh. "Come now," he said, "do you really think that you can put this big ocean in this little hole? Surely you can see that it is impossible? You may as well stop child, because you will never get it done!"

The boy threw away his little container and sternly looked at the bishop.

"Do you really believe that your limited mind can understand the eternal God? How could you ever hope to transfer the eternal God to your small world of thought? You had better stop trying. It is all in vain. Go home, my lord bishop, learn to believe like a child and never seek understanding beyond that of which you are able!"

No sooner had the boy finished speaking when he spread the wings attached to his back, and before the eyes of the astonished Augustine, he flew into the distance.

Augustine remained there for a long time, as though he were nailed to the spot.

He looked at the hole the boy had dug, and then he looked at the sea. He repeated the words the child had spoken and began to understand their meaning.

Walking home he sighed, "Lord, I thank Thee for sending this little boy. I realize he came from Thee, and I also understand what it was he had to teach me. I must never seek an answer to the mystery, "Who art Thou?" because I shall never be able to find it. Thou art far too great to be understood by me, a mere mortal man."

Once and for all, Augustine had learned that even the greatest human mind is incapable of comprehending the greatness of God.

That is what this lovely legend teaches us.


## CHAPTER SIXTEEN

# WAR IN THE LAND

The journey Augustine made in the company of his friend Alypius was long and tiring. The bishop was now seventy years old and weary. The journey from Hippo to Thubunae in the south of Numidia was certainly not easy at that age.

Why then make the journey?

He was being driven by his concern for the Christian Church. The Roman government had installed a soldier named Boniface as Lord Protector of North Africa, and he resided in Thubunae.

Something terrible had happened. In the spring of A.D. 427, Genserik, king of the Vandals and Alans, had crossed the strait of Gibraltar and advanced through North Africa, destroying everything in his path. The Christian Churches were the special target of his enterprise. He had heard that some of them were very rich, and he was after their treasures.

Refugees arrived in Hippo day after day, telling gruesome stories of attack and plunder that caused great depression among its citizens. However, this

did not impress the old bishop. It was not knowledge of atrocities that worried him, but what the outcome of those atrocities might be.

It seemed very possible that after three centuries of diligent labour, the African churches would perish–vanish!

As Augustine did not seem impressed when he heard the terrible tales of plunder and murder, most people thought that he did not really care about what could happen to them. But that was not true. On the contrary! In order to prove that they were wrong, he made the arduous journey to Thubunae. He wanted to encourage Boniface to take up the sword in defense of the country, and in particular, of the Christian Church.

When he finally reached his destination, he implored Boniface to take up arms immediately and not wait any longer to see what would happen.

What was the Lord Protector's reply?

"These worldly affairs lost their appeal to me a long time ago. I am seriously thinking of entering a monastery."

Augustine was very surprised indeed. Boniface had always enjoyed going to war. He had even used his privileged position to further his own ends. He had always lived a rather happy-go-lucky life. Did he now really want to convince Augustine that he was going to enter a monastery? The bishop pointed out the folly of such an attitude. Boniface was a soldier, and it was his duty to defend the country. He should not make the people think that it was impossible to serve God as a soldier!

Had not David, Cornelius, and many others been God-fearing soldiers?

Boniface seemed impressed by Augustine's words and quickly promised to do what the bishop asked. Greatly relieved, Augustine and Alypius went back to Hippo.

Boniface had no intention of keeping his word. He did not lift a finger to try to halt the aggressor. As a result, the country was systematically plundered.

Nothing was left. It had all gone as Augustine had predicted!

This caused the old bishop much grief. It was impossible to make another perilous journey, so he decided to write the Lord Protector a letter. It was a forthright and very courageous letter in which he reminded Boniface of his duty.

The letter did no more good than the journey had done. In fact, when Italy sent troops to help fight

the aggressor, Boniface made things worse by call-
ing in the Vandals, who were only too willing to
come. They advanced into Numidia and soon
threatened Hippo.

Masses of inhabitants fled before the threatening
enemy. What made Augustine very angry indeed
was that many bishops and other spiritual leaders
fled even sooner and faster than the members of
their congregations. He believed that the church
would not remain in Africa if her leaders deserted
her. His advice was to remain in the place of call-
ing. If need be, he would die for his faith rather
than leave his congregation.

At long last Boniface began to regret his cowardly
attitude. He asked Genserik to take his troops and
leave Numidia, but the Vandal king had no intention whatsoever of doing that. Boniface had better
not make any demands or Genserik would teach
him a thing or two! To prove his intentions, he
went to war against Boniface and defeated him.
The Lord Protector knew of nothing better to do
than, together with his small band of Gothic merce-
naries, flee to Hippo and there go into hiding.

When Genserik heard that Boniface was in Hippo,
he lay siege to the city. This made things extremely
difficult for Augustine, whose house was filled to
capacity with refugees.

During the course of one of the meals, Possidius,
bishop of Guelma, fell victim to despair. But Augustine said, "Don't talk like that Possidius, I pray to
God every day to break Genserik's siege and deliver
Hippo. Should His will be otherwise, then I ask Him
that His servant be given the strength to do His will
or take me up to Him, away from this earth!"

Augustine carefully followed the events of battle.
When Boniface was victorious, he wrote him an

encouraging letter, pleading with him not to rely on his own strength but to praise God, to trust Him who gives courage and upholds His servants.

Augustine's prayers to be taken up from this earth would be heard much sooner than even he himself expected.

# CHAPTER SEVENTEEN

## TAKEN UP

During the third month of the siege, Augustine became ill with a high fever. This was caused by a contagious disease that the refugees had brought into the city.

It was the end of August, and the weather was hot and humid. The evenings brought no relief.

Augustine stayed in bed as soon as he realized that he was ill, but even there people would not leave him in peace. On one occasion someone brought people who were mentally disturbed and asked if Augustine would pray for them. Augustine did pray, and the Lord heard his prayer; the sick people recovered.

This news soon travelled through the city, and before long, everyone brought their sick to his bedside. One of them told the old bishop that he had had a dream in which someone had told him, "Bring your sick to Augustine, and he will lay his hands upon the sufferer and he shall recover."

"My son," said Augustine, "you can see for yourself how ill I am. If I could really heal the sick, would I not heal myself first?"

However, he did pray, and the person was healed.

Augustine's own illness became worse every day and he pleaded to be left to prepare for death. After that, no one except the doctor and those who cared for him came to his bedside.

While he lay there, his whole life passed before him, and he pleaded with God to forgive all the sins he had committed.

Ten days he quietly waited for death. On September 5, he had a severe relapse.

Possidius and some of his most loyal friends stood around his bed. Reverently they sang some psalms, Augustine softly singing with them, "My soul thirsts for God, for the living God. Oh, when shall I behold His countenance?" And a little while later, "He Who is life came down to earth. He suffered our death through the greater part of His life. That life has come down to you—and you would not go up to it and live?"

Slowly Augustine's eyes clouded over and his features relaxed. Possidius bent over him. Augustine had been taken up from this world to the world of light and love, of peace and eternal joy.

Augustine was one of the greatest among the Church Fathers. He did much to combat false teachings, especially those of Pelagius, a monk who came from Ireland in A.D. 411, who taught that man at birth is good. Augustine, with the Bible in his hand, showed that man is corrupt from birth. It is not the desire of man to do good, that saves sinners but only Christ's atoning work!

We are grateful to the Lord for giving the church a man like Augustine. It is regrettable that after his death the church was corrupted and became Roman Catholic.

Many centuries later it was a farmer's son from Mansfield—Martin Luther—who would continue the work of the farmer's son from Tagaste and return to the people the infallible Word of God.

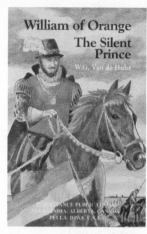

## William of Orange - The Silent Princ[e]
### by W.G. Van de Hulst

Whether you are old or young you will enjoy this biograph[y] on the life of William of Orange. Read it and give it [a]s a birthday present to your children or grandchildre[n]. A fascinating true story about one of the greatest princ[es] who ever lived and already by his contemporaries just[ly] compared to King David.

**Time: 1533-1584**       **Age: 7-9**
**ISBN 0-921100-15-9**       **US$11.9[5]**

## Struggle for Freedom Series
### by Piet Prins

David Engelsma in the *Standard Bearer*: This is reading for Reformed children, young people, and (if I am any indication) their parents. It is the story of 12-year-old Martin Meulenberg and his family during the Roman Catholic persecution of the Reformed Christians in The Netherlands about the year 1600. A peddlar, secretly distributing Reformed book[s] from village to village, drops a copy of Guido de Brès' *True Christian Confessio[n]* — a booklet forbidden by the Roman Catholic authorities. An evil neighbor see[s] the book and informs . . .

**Time: 1568-1573**       **Age: 10-9[9]**

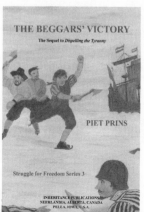

**Vol. 1** *When The Morning Came*
**ISBN 0-921100-12-4 US$11.95**

**Vol. 2** *Dispelling the Tyranny*
**ISBN 0-921100-40-X US$11.95**

**Vol. 3** *The Beggars' Victory*
**ISBN 0-921100-53-1 US$11.95**

**Vol. 4** *For the Heart of Holland*
**978-1-894666-20-6 US$12.95**

**SET OF 4 STRUGGLE
for FREEDOM Series
REG. 48.80
Special Set Price
US$41.49**

## The Lion of Modderspruit by Lawrence Penning
### The Louis Wessels Commando #1

A wonderful historical novel in which Penning has interwoven love, pathos, and loyalty. The conflict the Boers endure with England involves not only a fight to maintain their independence (to which the British agreed in 1881) but also a deep religious significance. Louis Wessels, eldest son of a well-established Transvaal Boer family, is betrothed to Truida, a Boer maiden living in the British colony of Natal, and educated in British-governed schools. When England sends over thousands of troops to invade the independent Boer colony of the Orange Free State, causing the Boers of the Transvaal Colony to prepare to invade Natal, the two lovers are confronted by more than a political conflict — two loyal hearts separated by loyalty

to conflicting causes. The horrors of the war drag both Louis and Truida through heights of joy and depths of despair. How can these two hearts, beating strongly for each other but also strongly for their separate causes, ever be reconciled? On which side is justice to be found?

| | |
|---|---|
| Time: 1899 | Age:11-99 |
| ISBN 1-894666-91-7 | US$10.95 |

## Zarco, the Explorer by K. Norel

Zarco signs on as mate apprentice aboard the fleet of Bartholomew Diaz who discovers the Cape of Good Hope. Under Vasco da Gama, Zarco later sails to India. Norel was one of Hollands best-loved authors of historical fiction.

| | |
|---|---|
| Time: 1441 - 1502 | Age: 12-99 |
| ISBN 0-88815-877-7 | US$10.90 |

## The Carpenter of Zerbst by P de Zeeuw, J.Gzn
### A Story from the Time of the Great Reformation

Join Otto's family as they cling to God's promises through all their grief and tension. Witness with joy the work of God in the lives of His children as well as in the lives of the enemies of the cross.

Another historical novel by P. de Zeeuw. Written in a fascinating way for children to learn church history. It will encourage them to remain steadfast in the faith and to confess with Martin Luther:

**Here I stand!**
**I cannot do otherwise.**
**May God help me! Amen.**

| | |
|---|---|
| Time: 1517-1522 | Age: 9-99 |
| ISBN 978-1-894666-34-8 | US$9.95 |

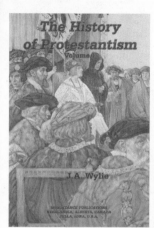

# The History of Protestantism
## by J.A. Wylie
### With hundreds of Original Classic Illustrations

The History of Protestantism is no mere history of dogmas. The teachings of Christ are the seeds; the modern Christendom, with its new life, is the good tree which has sprung from it. The author tells of the seed and also of the tree, small at first, still growing, and destined one day to cover the earth.

How that seed was deposited in the soil; how the tree grew up and flourished despite the furious tempests that warred around it; how, century after century, it lifted its top higher in heaven, and spread its boughs wider around, sheltering liberty, nursing letters, fostering art, and gathering a fraternity of prosperous and powerful nations around it. The author writes that the History of Protestantism is the record of one of the grandest dramas of all time.

It is true, no doubt, that Protestantism, strictly viewed, is simply a principle. It is not a policy. It is not an empire, having its fleets and armies, its officers and tribunals, wherewith to extend its dominion and make its authority be obeyed. It is not even a Church with its hierarchies, and synods and edicts; it is simply a principle. But it is the greatest of all principles. It is a creative power. Its plastic influence is all-embracing. It penetrates into the heart and renews the individual. It goes down to the depths and, by its omnipotent but noiseless energy, vivifies and regenerates society. It thus becomes the creator of all that is true, and lovely, and great; the founder of free kingdoms, and the mother of faithful churches. The globe itself it claims as a stage not too wide for the manifestation of its beneficent action; and the whole domain of terrestrial affairs it deems a sphere not too vast to fill with its spirit, and rule by its law.

—Adapted from the first chapter

**Vol. 1 ISBN 978-1-77298-020-2          US$48.90**
**Vol. 2 ISBN 978-1-77298-021-9          US$48.90**
**Vol. 3 ISBN 978-1-77298-022-6          US$48.90**

## Set of Three Large Hardbound Volumes US$124.90